SAVE ME, DOLLY PARTON

A MONOLOGUE

BY MEGAN GOGERTY

This play is dedicated to my mother,
who is tired of me writing plays about her.

Also Available By
Megan Gogerty

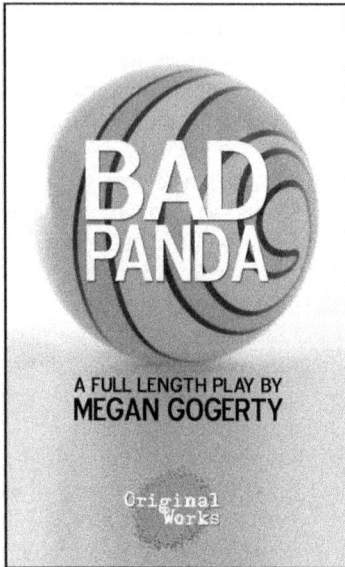

BAD PANDA

Synopsis: They're the last two pandas on earth. It's mating season. One of them falls in love with a crocodile. Who is gay. And then the baby comes. In this sweet celebration of non-traditional families, Gwo Gwo the panda must balance his newfound desire for Chester the crocodile with his obligations to his prescribed panda mate, Marion. The animals eat, mate, splash around in identity politics, wrestle with the ambivalence of parenthood, and love one another as only families can.

Cast Size: 2 Males, 1 Female

Character

Megan. W, 30s. Friendly and kind of a spaz.

SET AND TECHNICAL ELEMENTS

Set: A more-or-less bare stage. Two kitchen step stools, preferably of different heights, that get moved around quite a bit. Perhaps there is also a window with curtains, out of which a person might gaze wistfully.

Notes

There is one intermission, useful for selling things like beer and season passes.

Running time is approximately 90 minutes (45 minutes per act.)

Save Me, Dolly Parton (originally entitled Feet First In The Water With A Baby In My Teeth) received a rolling world premiere in 2011 with productions at Riverside Theatre (Iowa City; Artistic Director Jody Hovland) and Synchronicity Theatre (Atlanta; Artistic Director Rachel May). Alexis Chamow directed both productions.

SAVE ME, DOLLY PARTON

(Megan takes the stage. She wears a dress. She looks very nice and also non-threatening, and perhaps a little like a retro '50s housewife, although not so much it looks costume-y. She smiles warmly.)

MEGAN

So I have this kid. At the time of this story, he's three months old, a baby, and I am in love. He's a big baby – I mean big. Fat, tall, he has girth. He looks like Winston Churchill. He lies there on his back, waving his little fists, denouncing the Nazis.

Since he was born 12 weeks ago, I've been at home taking care of him. If I worked in an office, we'd call that "maternity leave." But since I'm a writer, it's just life. The baby spends all day eating and sleeping and passing gas, and I do the same.

But then I get a phone call – a job offer. Come to New York, do a thing, we'll pay you money. Not a lot of money, but a gig's a gig. So my husband and I sit down and ask ourselves, What do we do with the kid?

In the next three years, this question will come to dominate our lives.

We work through the logistics. Husband can't skip work. He just took a bunch of time off when the baby was born. The grandparents live too far away. Plus, the baby's breastfeeding, and I plan to take my breasts with me when I go.

So what? I'll just bring him along! He's portable. Did you know airlines let babies fly free? They gotta sit on your lap so they don't take up a seat, but still! Free! And strollers and car seats? They don't count as checked bags. They're considered mobility aids, so they're free. AND, I can bring a diaper bag on board and it doesn't count as one of my carry-ons. The airlines have the greatest customer service ever!

We get to the airport. I check a suitcase, the stroller, the car seat. I've got the baby strapped to my chest, like in a papoose thing. Purse, diaper bag, backpack, baby. It's like the baby's going on a trek across the desert. I'm the camel!

We go from Iowa to Chicago, Chicago to New York. The first leg of the trip is fine. Airport security? Fine. Flight to Chicago? Fine. Baby is laughing and having a great time. He's super cute, all the women on the flight give him googly eyes. I feel like a genius.

The second leg of the trip is longer. Baby is restless. We get in the air, and he starts to fuss. He keeps moving around. What with the seat back in front of me and the armrests where they are, there's not a lot of room for him on my lap. I try to stretch him out diagonally, but it's not working.

He's a big baby. He was ten pounds when he was born, and since then he's just been eating this whole time, so now he's – what? Thirteen pounds? Let me bring that home for you. Imagine you're in an airplane, and on your lap is a small to medium-sized Thanksgiving turkey. Who's mad at you.

When babies cry... Here's the good news. When babies cry, it's straightforward. They're hot, they're wet, they're hungry, it's like one of five things. The baby's not crying because of the economy. You just go through the checklist until you find the thing. Then you fix it.

But the thing is, a baby's cry is...*difficult* to listen to. We are evolutionarily designed to hate that sound. When you hear a baby crying, your first impulse is to do whatever you have to do to get it to stop making that sound. It's a klaxon, and the longer it goes on, the harder it is to think straight, or stay calm, or fix the problem. Fix the problem!

Is he hungry? Maybe he's hungry. I fish out my boob. I used to think that when in public, I would want to drape a cloth for modesty, but let's not kid ourselves. This baby is so big, to cover him I'd need a quilt. And anyway, once he latches on, nobody can see anything. It just looks like I'm wearing a very fancy brooch. Made of baby.

He spits out my boob. I offer it to him again. He spits it out again. He freaks out, I mean freaks! Limbs akimbo, red-faced, the whole she-bang.

You know those sit-coms with the perfectly swaddled baby in the arms of beautiful people, and all the beautiful people gather 'round and do something cute like, *(sings)* "Good night, sweetheart, well it's time to go!" and the baby just falls asleep? That is a lie. That does not happen. This baby is a pterodactyl. This baby is a tiny thunder god who is displeased. I have a flailing, caterwauling Thanksgiving turkey, and it is my job to shut him up. Shut up, Turkey!

The two people sitting next to me – oh, we're in a middle seat – have politely turned their faces away. The man on my left? Turkey has been kicking him in the thigh for twenty minutes.

I try bouncing, patting, swaddling, rocking. Nothing! It's gotta be the diaper. Right? I mean, what else is there? I grab the diaper bag and haul ass to the back of the plane.

Look. I know nobody likes to be on a plane with a crying baby. I know that's one of the circles of hell. I have been on a plane with a crying baby, and I have thought black thoughts.

But believe me when I tell you: as bad as you are suffering, sitting on that plane listening to that sound, the woman with the baby is suffering more. "Hi! Sorry! - shut up shut up shut up – he's really fussy for some reason! – shut up shut up shut up – excuse me, sorry, really sorry – shut up shut up please shut up they're going to kill us, they're going to throw us off this plane, shut up!"

We get in the little toilet closet and shut the folding door. There's barely enough room for us to turn around. There's no changing table. We can't have a changing table on a plane. The terrorists could use them to change their babies! There's no counter. I have to balance him on the toilet. Of course he is far too big, so I support his head with one hand and begin my crash course in one-handed diaper changing. And the baby is not lying there quietly, taking it. The baby is freaking out.

The problem is, Turkey here is sick and tired of being on a plane. He wants to go home. He wants to lie in his bed, somewhere familiar. But we're stuck. *(To the baby.)* Yes! Aren't we stuck! We're stuck in a metal box somewhere over Ohio!

We careen back to our seats. Turk is so distraught, he knocks my glasses off my face into somebody's lap. They hand them back to me like a dirty Kleenex. All the women making googly eyes? Nobody's making any googly eyes. We are pariahs, Turk and me.

The flight lands, and we take off toward baggage claim, Turk not letting up for an instant. I catch a glimpse of myself in a window, I look like a crazy person. My hair is standing straight up, I have all these bags hanging off me. I look like I just robbed a luggage store.

We get to the carousel, and I am lasered into it, mentally sucking the bags through the conveyor belt. The suitcase. The stroller. Car seat, car seat, where is the car seat? See, the baby's too young to sit in the stroller, he has to sit in the car seat that sits in the stroller, so I have to get the car seat. Car Seat Car Seat Car Seat...

Then finally it appears! Some helpful airline attendant has wrapped it in plastic. Not Saran Wrap, not a regular plastic bag, but industrial strength, military-grade, Al-Qaeda-proof tarp plastic. And then duct taped it.

So I am standing in the middle of the baggage claim surrounded by a ring of my bags, this ruddy fire alarm strapped to my chest, trying to open this package. I can't bend over, or the baby will fall out of the papoose thing. I can't put the baby on the ground in this filthy New York airport, so I am squatting and ripping into this thing with my teeth! *(Demonstrates.)* Through some Herculean force of strength I manage to get the sucker open, I stick the baby in the car seat, the baby goes *(big sigh)* … and falls asleep immediately.

And I start to cry. Because it's not over. I have to put the car seat in the stroller and then get all the bags and get a taxi and put the car seat into the taxi then I have to go to Queens to the fifth-floor walk-up where I'm staying that has no elevator, and this stroller is enormous! It has, like, sixteen cup-holders! It seemed like such a great idea when we got it but now it just seems ludicrous that something this big exists to cart around a baby, and how the hell am I going to get it on the subway? And I'm alone! There's only me!

And it's not just this trip. It's every trip. Every new excursion, every step forward is going to be this! Is going to look and feel like this! Weighted down by all this freight, with this person! With needs! That I cannot always anticipate or fulfill but I gotta find a way, I gotta do the impossible! It's my job now!

And I think, Whatever happened to feminism? I thought feminism had solved this problem. Do I need more feminism? I thought I had enough, but no! I need to join the Feminism club, I need to renew my Feminism subscription, I need to go to Amazon.com and type in Feminism and then click Add To Cart. Whatever it takes! Because feminism is supposed to make you feel liberated.

How do people do it? I see them do it. People walking around, having babies and living their lives like it's no big deal. I know it's possible.

Especially now. We have so many advantages now. We're living in the future. Modern times! We have science. We have epidurals and latex pacifiers and papoose-things. We have rights, and child labor laws, and casual Fridays.

And some people have twins! That's two separate babies at the exact same time! And this has been going on forever. People! Having babies! Cave people had babies. A hundred years ago, people in covered wagons and, like, really long dresses were having and raising babies. Pushing out ten, twelve kids, then churning butter and, like, pickling things. With all their babies just around.

But they did it, those women. With far fewer privileges, they did it successfully for hundreds of years. We don't even have to go back that far. My own mother didn't have squat. She grew up on a chicken farm, slaughtering chickens.

Funny story: Here's how you kill a chicken. There's actually a couple different methods. Some people recommend the butcher knife, that's where you hold the chicken down and then cut its head off, but it's messy. Blood gets everywhere, on your smock, it's disgusting. And it takes two people, one to hold the chicken down and the other to kill it. And if you're a nine-year-old girl responsible for slaughtering a bunch of these things on your own, it's just not practical. There's a far more efficient method.

You take a really stiff wire – a straightened out coat hanger is perfect – and you attach one end to a broom handle like you would a wire to a fence post – say a staple, or a U-nail. Something. Then with the other end of the wire, you bend that into a big hook. And you snake this along the ground, and this is what you use to capture the chicken. You jerk it toward you. It's like a horrible death vaudeville.

So you got this chicken and you grab it by its feet and hold it upside down. And this causes the chicken to get very still. Chickens are not the brightest creatures. They know they're in mortal danger, but they don't know what to do about it. So they think if they're still enough, you won't notice they're a chicken.

So you've got this thing by the feet, and then you gently lay the chicken's head on the ground, then you step on it. This does not kill the chicken. We are not Riverdancing our chickens to death. But it pins it to the ground really good. So you got your foot on the chicken's head. And you've got a good grip on this thing's feet, and that's when you go, "One Two Three!" *(Yank. Throws chicken aloft.)*

Blood geysers out of the neck! And the chicken flops around, and if they flop in the right direction, they'll catch their feet and run for a bit. If there's any air in the caught in the windpipe, it'll emit a high-pitched whining or perhaps keening sound. Like a balloon leaking air. *(Demonstrates. Chicken collapses.)* Then while it's real fresh, you dunk it in a vat of hot water to loosen the feathers. Then you pluck it, gut it, and get it butchered.

Boy, if that doesn't make you want to go to college.

The chicken farmers, who were not her biological family, they just raised her from the age of seven, didn't think a girl needed education. But she wormed her way into high school and then snuck her way into a scholarship, and she never went back to that chicken farm again.

My childhood memories of my mother are all that of grim exhilaration. She was a relentless locomotive, barreling her way toward her goals. A single parent, she raised three kids on a teacher's salary, no grandparents, no relatives to baby-sit. And not only did she cook and clean and pay the bills, she went night school. She earned her masters, then her doctorate, never taking out a loan, paying for it all one class at a time. It took her eleven years.

That's the thing about killing chickens – everything else is easy by comparison.

And where did she learn this drive, this will to succeed? From the women who came before her, of course. From her grandmother who raised her until her death, Grandma Ronan.

Grandma Ronan ran a boarding house in her older years, but when she was sixteen, she worked in a kitchen on a steamboat on the Mississippi River. She'd had her baby by then – paternity uncertain – and made her way scrubbing out pots and pans. The story goes, one night there was a fire on the boat. Grandma Ronan couldn't swim, had never been in water deeper than a bathtub, but she grabbed that baby and jumped overboard feet first, where she dogpaddled a good half mile to shore, all the while clutching that baby in her teeth by the diaper.

Can you imagine being that baby? You're hanging out, doing your baby thing. You're on a steamboat, so it's not like you're in a well-appointed nursery. You're probably in a dresser drawer. But it's cool, you're a baby. And then suddenly you're flying through the air, all this noise and commotion, then you're in the river, which is cold and muddy, waves hitting you in the face, getting a colossal diaper wedgie. For a half mile.

And let's talk about the neck muscles on my great-grandmother. A baby is a good seven to ten pounds or so. Are you gonna lift ten pounds by your teeth and swim across the Mississippi River? And you know that baby's not being exactly coop-erative. He's not saying, "Hey, mom, I can see you're in the middle of something here, why don't I just hold still and let you take care of business, and when you're finished saving both our lives, maybe you can attend to some of my needs? When you get a sec, no rush. I can see this has been a very stressful night for you, you might need a little You Time."

No, she muscled that kid over the waves through sheer will. Who does that? How does somebody do that?

But when I ask my mother, she tells me the same thing: You figure it out. You just get in there and wing it. And women like my great-grandmother did it with no money and no help – hell, she didn't even have the right to vote.

This is my lineage. All these women, stretching back to forever, scraping by. Their whole life's work amounted to nothing but pennies in a jar. But like pennies in a jar, it kept accruing, passed up and up through the generations. So by the time it got to me, it was heavy and full and I was rich!

(Sudden samba music.) I went to college! I shop at Costco! I have a Roomba! I check my email and get a little yawny around nine o'clock

because I've had such a hard day. I am blessed – no. Not blessed. I am loaded.

I grew up confident that the only limits on me were self-imposed. I could grow up to do anything I wanted. I could be an astronaut. I could be an artist.

I could be Dolly Parton!

Dolly Parton is the… I don't want to overstate. Dolly Parton is simply the greatest woman alive. For pity's sake, she wrote "9 to 5" on her fingernails! *(Demonstrates.)* And listen to this lyric: "Tumble out of bed, stumble to the kitchen. Pour myself a cup of ambition." That's clearly genius! Not just the rhyme, but the pairing of "kitchen" with "ambition" thematically... I mean, men tumble out of bed and drink coffee in the morning too, but you'd never see that rhyme in a song about a man.

The first time she came into my life, I was in college. I was preparing to go on a road trip with my boyfriend in his jalopy of a car. How old was this car? It had a tape deck. Talk about Antiques Roadshow. We were going to drive twelve hours to Alliance, Nebraska to pay homage to Car-henge. It's a local art sculpture, an exact to-scale replica of Stonehenge, only with cars. We thought it sounded kitchy and stupid, so we were fired up about it. It's the kind of kitchy, stupid thing you do in college, drive a solid day in a crappy car for the privilege of feeling superior.

And our music! Our music made us feel worldly, which is quite a trick, since neither of us had ever left Iowa. We felt sophisticated, my boy-friend and I. We didn't go to football games and get drunk. We went to rock shows and got drunk. We went to fencing demonstrations and DIY craft fairs. We were smart and privileged and in on the joke.

And we were young. Marvelously so.

To prep for my road trip, I went to this place called a Record Store. I was looking for groaners, you know? Terrible, ridiculous music. Kitchy. Stupid. Camp.

They had this barrel in the back full of these old cassettes that were on clearance – four bucks a pop. I found some real gems in there. Some truly silly haircuts.

And then – the masterpiece.

There she was, splayed out on the cover of this thing. She looked like a clown. This too-blonde wig, these curls, these painted lips and nails. Oh, and of course – the boobs. Who on earth could take this woman seriously?

The tape had maybe 10 songs on it. I showed my boyfriend the cover art before we left the driveway. We howled.

And then we put the tape in.

We played side A, then side B. Then side A. Then side B. Then side A. We couldn't turn it off. The rolling farmland of Iowa melted into the flinty rock of western Nebraska and still we couldn't turn it off. We tried, once. Got through a song and a half of the old stuff before we both agreed to eject it and go back to the first tape. We didn't want to break the spell.

It was her early stuff, we found out later. Her hits from the '70s. It was like music from another world to us, because it was.

You've got to understand, nobody we knew listened to country music. Country music was for rubes and rednecks and racists. There was music, and then there was country music.

And it wasn't just the demographic stuff, either. Country music, to my ear, was terrible. I mean genuinely terrible music. With those hokey poky fiddles and put-on twangs and achy-breaky hearts? It was like a costume party.

But this! This was different. Her twang wasn't store-bought, it wasn't phony. It was just her natural voice – her mountain stream of a plaintive croon. High and sweet, it cut through the din and fog. Even on the crappy car stereo speakers, she rang out with chilling clarity. Songs about love, and jealousy, and family and being poor and loving someone new after being kicked around and butterflies. Butterflies! And it all just felt so true and real. I recognized it. And it was like the scales fell from my eyes.

When we got to Carhenge, we walked around in a trance. We went looking for kitchy-stupid, but instead we found cock-eyed brilliance, holy ground. The cars were hoisted vertically, buried into the ground up to their windshields, looking majestic and intimidating. We paced around like American druids, dumbstruck, in wondrous awe.

Our friends back home did not get it. But I didn't care. Something had shifted in me with this music. Here was this woman, coming up from hardscrabble beginnings, who made this simple music about adult problems. And she was doing it during a time when married women couldn't get their own credit cards. When marital rape was still legal. When being pregnant while on the job was in itself a fire-able offense. She did it. On her terms.

Her original 1974 version of "I Will Always Love You"? I dare you to listen to it without breaking into tears. No, forget Whitney Houston. Please. The way Dolly does it, it's simple and direct. When I'm having a bad day, I turn the lights down, I put on her music, and she makes me feel better. I can't explain it. Even when I'm at my lowest, Dolly Parton pulls me up and inspires me. It's like she understands.

And my boyfriend? Well. We had to get married after that. How could we not get married, after the Dolly Awakening?

We decide to start a family, and it's easy. Natural. I've got a husband who loves Dolly Parton - and also me. I have a burgeoning career, a supportive partner, a life, and I want to share that life with a child, I want to show him all the beautiful things in the world. Husband and I walk hand in hand into that bright future, smiling, eyes open, armed with education, supported by the belief we are ready for anything.

See, where a lot of parents go wrong is, they're not organized. They let the baby-ness overtake them. That's why I bought seven diaper bags – well, two of them were gifts. A large one, a medium-large one, an extra-large one, a small one that will live in the car and is eternally stocked, and then this regular one for everyday, which I'll keep by the door. Then when it's time to leave, you don't have to hunt for things. You just scoop it up.

Here's the other thing I did: I made a flowchart. For CPR. Because if your baby needs CPR, who's going to remember, you know, how many chest compressions? But this takes all the guesswork out of it. You just go to the flowchart. I got a flowchart for choking, a flowchart for swaddling, for how to launder cloth diapers – well, it's less a flow chart and more a decision tree. Here's my favorite: a flow chart for crying! It was husband's idea to put magnets on the back of this one. We'll just stick it to the fridge next to poison control. And then when we're like, "Oh no, baby's crying, we're new parents, what'll we do?" Flow chart.

The flow charts are a great idea. I got it from this book, *Welcoming Baby Home*. I got a book on sleeping, a book on eating, this book is just general parenting. This book is about how to have fun with your baby – in case you forget.

And look, this one lays out for you a typical baby's day. What time they eat, when they nap. They nap all the time. It's perfect – when the baby's napping, that's when I'll do my work! The house will be quiet. It's ideal.

In my 20th week of pregnancy, I go to the doctor, and the Ultrasound says it's a boy. *(Disappointed face.)* That's fine. I read in this book, boys are just like regular people. I can raise a boy. The world needs more non-sexist, cool boys. *(Gasps.)* What if he's gay? Please be gay! I would be the best mother to a gay son. We'd play dress up. We'd get our colors done. If you are a gay baby being born in Iowa, this is the one you want. Think I could gay up his room at all? I mean, I know it's nature, not nurture, but still. I could hang up a couple Liza Minnelli posters.

Either way, I got this. Husband and I, we have got this!

(Exciting 1920s-style party music.) Won't it be great when he gets here! Think of the fun we'll have. We'll go to art museums. We'll travel the world!

The baby year flashes by. Standing here now, I can barely remember it. I just have this sensory blur of sleep deprivation, diaper changing, and cuddling this soft, milk-fed little animal.

Mother Nature is very smart. She gives you this infant, this child, wholly dependent on you, with these big eyes and perfect mouth, and you fall in love with this creature. Head over heels. And it's good, and it's right, because if you didn't love your baby so deeply, so purely, to your bones, when he grows into a toddler, you would kill him. You would lock him in a closet with some Cheetos and a DVD and hit the road. You would change your name and sell jewelry on the side of the highway, if that's what it takes.

You need that first beautiful baby year to cement your bond, because he starts walking and talking and fighting and he won't put on his pants, and you cajole and you nag, and you reason, and you wrestle him to the floor, and still no pants! Put your pants on! Pants! On! Put your pants on!

And I think, at least we're in it together. Husband and me. True partners, fifty-fifty on all the big decisions. We start out great. And then something happens.

When I was pregnant, we got all this pressure to breastfeed. You're gonna breastfeed, aren't you? You know, breast is best! It's less expensive than formula and healthier! If you breastfeed, the baby gets all these immunities! If you breastfeed, the baby will have less gas! If you breastfeed, you'll lose weight super fast, you'll be a skinny, sexy mama, how's that sound? Sounds good, doesn't it? So, you gonna breastfeed? You gonna breastfeed? You're gonna breastfeed, aren't ya? You're gonna breastfeed?

And husband and I were like, "Pssh! Of course we're gonna breastfeed! You had us at 'less expensive'!"

And then we have the baby. And a baby needs to eat every couple of hours. But that's okay, 'cause I got the milk right here!

And when the baby cries, the first step is to give it to the mama, who's got the milk. And the mama becomes the expert on the baby. He's not hungry, he's tired. He's got gas. He's too hot in this coat, you gotta take the coat off.

And the other parent, he's in there doing it – he's changing diapers, he's giving the baby a bath, he's bonding with the baby. But he doesn't have the boobs. And eventually, through nobody's fault, that parent becomes the daddy. And the mama is in charge.

And now a precedent has been set. As the kid grows up, he skins his knee, he wants his mama. He gets scared at night, he wants his mama. He loves his daddy, but he needs his mama. Mama is on point. Mama is the primary caregiver.

Mama is me.

Husband and I, after years of road trips and candlelight dinners, it's like we're not even married anymore. We're like business partners. Ninety percent of our conversation is logistics. "Listen, I got a meeting, you need to take off work early and watch him. Well, I can't do it, I got a thing I have to do, they're counting on me. You can't do that, 'cause who's gonna watch the kid? Who's gonna take care of the kid? What'll we do with the kid?"

The kid dictates my schedule. My clothes must be kid-proofed. Even my body is unrecognizable.

About a month or so after Turk was born, I decide to leave the house for the first time. Get a little air. We need a few things at the grocery store, so Turk and I get a cart and we're leisurely going up and down the aisles. And it's nice, being out.

And we're browsing our way through the store, really taking our time, when it comes over me with a shocking immediacy. I am seized with the need to pee. A sudden, intense urinary urgency. I have to go and I have to go right now.

I dart around, looking for the bathroom, but I don't know where it is. Do you know where the bathroom is in your grocery store? I don't go to the bathroom at the grocery store! But I need to go. I need to go! I need to go! *(Gasp.)* I go!

I am pissing in the grocery store. The muscles that you use to hold it in are the same muscles you use to push the baby out and they are useless. I am urinating, I am peeing freely! Not just a little pee. Not just like ah-choo, and whoopsie! It's a flood. A waterfall of disaster. A whole two-liter of Diet Mountain Dew.

I squat down, I clutch the shelf for support, and the first thought I have is, thank God I'm wearing a skirt. It flares around my legs like a tent, and as long as I'm squatting here, no one can see the puddle. Maybe this is why women wear skirts in the first place! For just these emergencies!

What should I do? I have never been in this situation before. Should I call my husband? My cell phone is in my purse, which is way up there in the cart with the ticking time bomb that is my sleeping baby. Any second now, he could wake up, he could cry. I can't just squat here forever!

There's nothing for it. I'm going to have to run. Wait till the coast is clear, then take the baby and get out. Clean up in aisle four! Oh, God!

My heart is racing, but I'm breathing, I'm getting focused, I'm white-knuckling this shelf waiting for my moment to speed out of here, and hope nobody notices my skirt is a little damp, when it gradually comes to my awareness: the shelf I'm squatting in front of, that I'm currently eye-level with, is a shelf of Depends.

I take baby and run. Nobody stops me. There goes the mama. Skinny, sexy mama.

Is this what motherhood is? Squatting in a grocery store in a puddle of humiliation? No. Surely this is a fluke, a low watermark in an ever-fluctuating tide of experience. So I peed my pants. It's not like I've never done it before! Granted, I was in preschool.

But what bothers me is, why didn't someone tell me about this? That this was even a possibility? I don't remember seeing the chapter in the "What To Expect" series on public urination! There was some talk about exercises you could do, various clutching-type exercises, but I thought those were just to get in ready for the birth, not for life after birth. Not for the grocery store.

Where were the cues? I'm used to cues! The pressure, the "Hey, pretty soon I've got to go" that you can plan. But this!

I've got to get control. Of my bladder, and my life. I've just got to work harder, be better. I mean, really, in the grand scheme of things, I'm glad this happened. I've had my one big surprise. Right?

INTERMISSION.

(Lights up. Her appearance has changed dramatically. Instead of a nice dress, she's wearing horrible sweatpants and a dirty, too-big t-shirt. Her lips are significantly less glossed.)

MEGAN

I'm a role model for Turk. Every woman he meets for the rest of his life, he'll view through the lens of my example. I've got to show him, Look, your mama loves you and nurtures you, but she also does this. She also works and writes and engages with the outside world. He's going to learn what a woman is from me. *(Picks nose, wipes on shirt.)*

I'm very careful. For example, I don't want to diet in front of Turk. I want to model for him a woman who is not made crazy by her body.

My sister once found herself having gained some weight, as happens from time to time. And she didn't have any pants that fit. So she went to the Gap, feeling really depressed. And the sales clerk was like, "Can I help you?" And my sister says, "Yeah, I don't know what size I wear. I just lost sixty pounds."

My sister is a genius.

But it worries me, what kind of man my boy will be. And what he'll think about women.

The other day, husband and I go to rent a movie. So here I am in this video store. And we're browsing the Comedy section, when I'm stopped by one particular image.

On the cover, in the foreground, there's a headless woman. You can't see her head, at any rate. She's splayed out across the cover, arms and legs tacked out from her torso like a dead moth. It should go without saying that she's in her under-wear. In the background are these fully clothed, unattractive man-boys, tongues wagging. And bla-zoned across this woman's taut, cartoon ass, is the title of the movie.

Now, I'm not naïve. I've seen this image before. We've all seen this image before. You know exactly what I'm talking about here. And sure enough, every row I look, my eyes land on some version of this image: A woman with her thumb tucked suggestively into the waistband of her panties, a woman swinging by her thong, which is caught on the tip of a naughty font. Standing in the Comedy section, I find myself flanked by an outpouring of boobs and butts and body parts.

And I'm watching my son, who is going up and down the aisles pulling all the videos off the shelf while my husband follows him around, putting them back, and watching him find glee in the chaos he creates, and I think, Thank God. Thank God he's a boy. He'll never have to be in this position. Yes, I'll have to teach him these women are cartoon women, and that real women are not here solely for his titillation, but at least he'll never be ogled. He'll never freak out about his body, feel like he has to live up to some impossible ideal. That's one good thing about boys, that's one bullet dodged.

But then I remember Abercrombie & Fitch. You know how most stores in the mall have store windows with their clothes displayed? No windows in Abercrombie & Fitch. It's all dark, and blazoned across the door, daring you to come in, are these giant pictures of naked men. Naked, chiseled, hairless men.

And one time, I'm at the mall and I pass the Abercrombie & Fitch store, and there's the naked men pictures. And there's a new one. There's a full-sized, full color picture of a shirtless man. He's standing there in a jacket, no shirt, and he's just oozing sex.

And it's such a dazzling photo that I stop in my tracks and take it in. It's one of those pictures where it looks like he's looking right at you, and he's a model so he's beautiful and young, and I'm just staring at this picture. Really observing it closely. The abs, the nipples, the jeans, giving the whole thing a frank assessment.

And then the picture goes like this *(wipes nose)* and oh my God, it's a real guy! They have hired some guy to stand there, and he and I have been having a staring contest for five minutes!

And oh no! He gets embarrassed, he turns red, he thinks I'm laughing at him! I'm not laughing at him at all, I'm laughing at me, for my apparent inability to tell a photo from real life.

I'm so flummoxed. I can't talk to him, but I want to show him I'm sorry or something, so I rush into the store. Like maybe it worked, his standing out there lured in a new customer. But it's all dark in there, and the music is pounding, and I feel like a trapped animal, so I rush back out again and keep going, and I don't slow down till I hit the pretzel stand.

I mean, how is that right? That man – young man, very young man – is somebody's son. Is my son going to feel like a failure if he doesn't look like a Greek god? You know they're never going to have some schlubby guy at Abercrombie & Fitch, standing around shirtless, trying to sell shirts. They're never going to have somebody who weighs in the 95th percentile.

My kid's in the 95th percentile. In weight. The doctor says, Uh-oh! But what's the problem? He's always been in the 95th percentile in weight.

(Doctor.) "Yes, but that was when he was in the 95th percentile in height AND weight. When a child begins to stray from their growth chart, we grow concerned. You see, here is the growth chart of a typical infant and toddler. This blue line is the 50th percentile, that means the average child weighs this much at this age. And this red line, this is the top of the curve. And you can see, we've been tracking Turk since he was born. Here's his very first weigh-in: Here's the blue line, the red line, and here's Turk! *(Gestures off the chart.)* And at three months: blue line, red line, Turk. Blue line, red line, Turk. And it's all been very consistent. But now, his height chart says blue line, red line. But his weight chart is still blue line, red line, Turk. Can you see? I think we should start transitioning away from the carbohydrates and towards the lean proteins, the chicken, more meat."

He doesn't like meat. He likes yogurt.

"Well. I think we need to start educating him on healthy food choices. Before it's too late."

He's two. Isn't he a little young for the Atkins Diet? He's not obese, he's roly-poly. I don't want the first thing he learns about himself to be that he's fat. Must we begin this worry? I do not want him to be Abercrombie. Or Fitch. I don't want him to have these anxieties, the awareness that comes from being constantly evaluated. I don't want him to feel like an object that has to live up to perfection. The world is messed up enough without that.

I have a website. And a few years ago, a friend of mine who's a photographer calls me up and says, I have this funny image in my mind of you getting hit in the face with a pie, let's take some pictures. And we do, and they turn out great, and they end up being the key images on my website. When you go to my website, you see me in a tie, and I'm running obliviously toward this cream pie. And then if you click on the "about me" page you'll see the After picture of me, covered in the pie.

And so I have these pictures on my website for a couple of years. And then one day I'm upgrading my site, and I get all these new tools that allow me to see how many hits per day my website is getting, and also how people are finding my website, what they're Googling for that brings them to me.

And I notice that among the list of my plays and other things, a common search term is "pie in the face." People are typing in "pie in the face" and finding me.

And I think, oh that's cute. What I don't understand is that "pie in the face" is a sexual fetish. There's a whole subset of people out there who enjoy seeing people – women – hit in the face with pies. It's a thing.

And a savvy person would see that people are Googling this and conclude, "Oh, this must be a porn thing." But I see it and conclude, "Oh! People must really like clowns! Vaudeville must be making a comeback!"

So I put out a call to my readers. "People seem really interested in pies in the face, so if you have a picture or a story of getting hit in the face with a pie, send it to me! I'll put it on my website!"

And I got some responses. And the responses make it clear they're not interested in clowns. And I start to suspect. So I go to Google and I type in "pie in the face, Megan Gogerty."

And there are all these chat rooms. So, so many chat rooms. All discussing me. And ranking my pie-in-the-face picture. And finding it wanting in certain respects. And offering to show me a real pie in the face. And heartened that I seemed so "open to it" with my call for submissions.

And I felt really weird. Like I accidentally made a porno.

I mean, here is my website that I have complete control over my image and my presentation, with these sexless, G-rated pictures, and it turns out I'm catering to this fetish community. And fine, you know, it takes all kinds, and have your fetish, I just didn't know about it. Which begs the question, what else don't I know?

How am I supposed to teach my son to safely navigate his own sexuality when I'm out there flaunting myself to the pie people? I don't want to make a mistake with him. I don't want to expose him to a danger without realizing it. As long as we're careful, we should be okay – as long as we don't watch any movies or read any books, or go anywhere, and avoid confusing things, like new people or experiences. We'll be fine. Right?

"Maybe you need to leave the house," my husband says to me one day. "You're getting kind of a weird look." No, I don't need to leave the house. I hate leaving the house. Turk is two and potty training, so it always feels like a gamble. We spend most of our days locked inside, relying on only each other for company.

My whole day is structured around Turk and his needs. Sometimes we don't even get out of our pajamas. When it was warm, we would go outside, maybe walk to the park, but now, when it's cold, our days bleed together in a morass of books and toys and Dora The Explorer. Sticky, leaky days.

My husband leaves for work in the morning and I envy him his lunch breaks, his mindless web surfing between projects at work. And I know the grass is always greener, he's looking at my day and wishing he could just kick around with his kid for a while and not put up with the stresses of being the primary breadwinner.

I remember watching sit-coms like *Full House*, you remember? With cool Uncle Jesse, played by John Stamos, who stays home with the kids and plays guitar and imparts life lessons while maintaining his perfectly styled hair. And it's the perfect job for a musician – play in your rock band at night and cuddle your kids during the day, who are cute and say funny things. And everyone – everyone! - has lots of energy.

The other day, I stepped in a pile of human excrement. In my house. It must have fallen out of a diaper. Or else he just pulled his pants down and expressed himself. I am walking in my sheepskin slippers, and squish.

I try to squeeze in my work whenever I can. There's a writing award I'm applying for – I've been a finalist a few years' running now. I can't say that my application this year is the strongest. I can't seem to find the blocks of time I need to concentrate. I think, Oh, I'll write during his naptime, but then it rolls around and I need a nap. I'm not meeting my deadlines. I need to do my work.

He hates my work. He hates my laptop. He sees it as a threat, which it is. He climbs on my lap and tries to push my computer off the couch. He bangs at the keys when I'm typing. I get up to answer the phone, when I come back, he's got his juice box aimed at the thing like a gun. "Turk, don't you dare. Don't. You put that down. Turk. Turk!"

I remember my books, my toddler books. They are chock full of helpful hints. Try to get down to his eye level. Try speaking in a baby voice! Mimic his tone, so he knows you're listening. Try getting his attention with a clap-clap-growl. You clap your hands together so he knows you mean business, then you growl like a dog. Toddlers are primal creatures. He'll respond to the pack leader in you.

"Turk! Turk! Turkey Sandwich! You get over here. You don't touch mama's computer. Do you hear me? Don't touch! *(clap-clap)* Don't! Touch! Mama's! Computer!" *(Growl.)*

The kid bursts. Fits of giggles. He laughs at me!

The rage…the rage I feel… I have to walk away. He follows me – this is a fun game. I go into the bathroom and lock the door. He freaks out, he can't reach me, he starts crying, pounds on the door, but I need a minute, I need a time-out – *(yelling.)* Mama needs a time-out! I am trying to calm my body. Breathe, breathe. He's really a lovely boy, he doesn't realize what he's doing. He's acting childish because he is a child, and this is a normal phase of growth, he's testing me. And I will not hit him. I will think about it, but I will refrain. And then I will eat several cookies. And I will not share them. And if he asks me what I'm eating I will tell him they are made of broccoli. And with this small revenge in mind, I can come out of the bathroom.

Maybe my husband's right. Maybe it would be good for Turk and I to get out of the house. Maybe I could do with some peers.

Our local library is having a story time for toddlers. This seems like a great idea. Other toddlers, other moms! Turk is resistant. He's a cautious gentleman, very slow to warm up to strangers. I fight a titanic battle to get him into his coat and the car, and then we're off.

The library is lovely – clean, colorful, very kid-friendly. The story time is happening in a reading room in the back. By the time we arrive, there are easily a dozen mothers and their spawn. Turk and I freeze at the doorway, mutually overwhelmed.

These women – who are these women? They look like alien creatures. Their hair is… combed. Not just combed; styled. Like, with products. Their clothes are neat, pressed. They're wearing make-up.

When the librarian shows up at the front with her books, all the kids kneel quietly to listen. She launches in on a story about a dog who throws a birthday party, but Turk is having trouble sitting still. He's not interested in the birthday party dog. I try to scoot him into my lap like I see the other mothers doing, but he's not into it.

"I have to go potty!" says Turk, so we scurry out of there. The restroom is right next-door, and it's great. Lots of room, and in addition to the full-size toilet, there's also a kid-sized commode right there, with handrails and everything. It's like a potty paradise.

"Isn't this nice?" I say. Turk is immediately suspicious. "I have to go potty!" he says, like maybe I didn't understand him the first time and have accidentally brought him into this cold, tiled room filled with toilets.

"There's the potty there, see? Let me help you with your pants." The noise starts small but grows, you can practically see it in his chest, a little bead of yellow panic gathering steam as it passes the lungs and finds voice in his nasal resonators: No-o-o-o!

"Turk, listen," I say, calmly, rationally, "This is the potty, you need to go potty, here it is." But toddlers are incapable of reason. I know I've got to cut this tantrum off at the pass, that's the key. If you let 'em accelerate into full tantrum, it'll be too late.

"You say no potty, Turk, is that right? You say no potty, no potty, mama!" But he's beyond language now, terror has gripped him at a visceral level. He and that commode are like Indiana Jones and the boulder, all he can think of to do is flee.

"You wanna go, honey, is that what you want? It's a fifteen-minute drive, Turk, can you hold it?" I should really put a diaper on him, a Pull-Up, but can you believe it, the diaper bag is out of Pull-Ups. Who takes a diaper bag without any diapers in it?

"Okay, honey, okay. Let's just pull up your pants and go, c'mon honey..." He is corkscrewing the floor like Donald O'Conner in *Singing In The Rain*, his pants bunched up around his ankles, screaming bloody murder. When he was a baby, I could just haul him out of there, but he's too big now, there's too much stuff. I yank his pants up with more force than I intend – he won't hold still, he thinks I'm going to frog-march him to the toilet – I try for the zipper, who puts a button-fly on a pair of toddler pants? My coat, his coat, our hats and gloves, I scoop everything up, clutching it like a homeless person with a bag of cans. I grab him by the wrist and muscle him to the door.

Standing outside the bathroom, rooted to the spot, are two small children from the story time. They've been waiting their turn like good little children, all in line, hands to themselves, and now they are staring at us, terrified. They heard the torture sounds coming from the bathroom. They think they might be next.

The children's mothers, also waiting patiently, stare into the middle distance. Their faces are as frosty as their highlights. What would it cost them, a sympathetic glance, an I've-been-there grimace? Is it too much to ask for a pat on the arm? Where's the sisterhood?

We should be surrounded by a crowd of other mothers with a whole passel of children at our feet. And one of us should be shelling peas, and another braiding hair, and another shepherding the children in and out of the garden. And the older kids look after the younger kids, and we're not alone in this. We should be living commune-style! Not this horrible isolation. Come on, ladies!

Who's with me? Surely I'm not the only one with a toddler in melt-down! A little sympathy? A little conviviality? Nothing?

Fine. Who needs you? Turk and I will just be Turk and I. Together, alone. Alone together. A boy and his mother! Like the Bates family! We don't need anybody else!

My own mother stops by the house later. "You look terrible. Your hair is a mess. Either get it cut, or get a perm." Mom, nobody gets perms anymore. "Well, you should. Something. You need to take care of yourself, make some friends. Get some exercise. Go to the gym. You're starting to lose it, Megan. You are losing it."

I opt for a step aerobics class. I didn't know they still had step aerobics. Didn't step aerobics go the way of the perm? But here we are.

The first thing I notice is that everyone in the room is about a half a foot shorter than I am. Brown hair, round shoulders, skin in various shades of tanning bed, wrinkled – it's like I'm in a room full of walnuts. I can't be friends with these women. I'm too tall. We march up and down on our steps like we're trapped in individual MC Escher paintings, and afterwards they lapse into talk about their grandchildren, and I just get out of there.

"They're forming book clubs at the library," my husband says. "Why don't you join a book club?" No. You have to do stuff like read the book. And you take turns bringing in snacks, it's too much.

"You could get a hobby," my sister says. "You've always wanted to learn to crochet. There's free lessons at the hobby store." Crochet? I'm not going to crochet! There's little hooks and yarn and you have to squint and just forget it.

What I need to do is write.

(Phone call.) "Megan, hi, it's Nancy! Listen, I'm so excited, I have amazing news. I won! The writing award! I got it!" Oh, Nancy, that's wonderful. "I can't believe it! A national award!" Nancy, seriously, you're so talented. You so deserve it. And hey, maybe you can put in a good word for me with the committee next year, huh? "Ohmigod, of course! Listen, I gotta go, I'm call-

ing everybody! Aah! I'm so excited!" I'm thrilled for you, Nancy, really. It couldn't have happened to a nicer person.

(Hangs up. A moment on the cusp of something bad. Rallies.)

Dolly Parton was born poor, dirt-floor poor, and the day she graduated from high school she drove to Nashville because she figured she couldn't get any poorer than she already was, and she slept in her car, pounding the pavement, knocking on doors. Until one day she got a break, she got a songwriting job. Then she became a regular on Porter Waggoner's nationally syndicated TV show, as the pretty little blonde girl singer until she started to build a following and she wanted to go solo, but the problem was she had signed these draconian contracts and Porter Waggoner had all the rights to her music and controlled what she recorded and when and when she tried to leave he took her to court and it was a messy, acrimonious, public split, almost like a divorce, but she wrested her way free and became a huge crossover sensation, and she wrote "I Will

Always Love You" as an apology to Porter Waggoner and she charted her own course and made her own money and she stayed true to herself and now she has a theme park! And she gives money to charity and she did it all, all of it, through sheer force of will and luck and stamina! She endured!

But she doesn't have any kids.

This is crazy. The other night he crawled into my bed in the middle of the night and I know this because he woke me up by sticking his fingers up my nose, and there are women, women who can't have babies, who desperately want a baby, who are dying for the fingers-in-the-nose experience. And I don't want to complain, I don't want to act resentful, I'm just so surprised! I find myself so completely surprised by how thoroughly he has eclipsed me. Where am I? I feel like I stumbled into a two-year-old hole, and it has swallowed me entirely! Why did I go to school, why did I work so hard, just to surrender it all so completely? What happened to me?

(Change. A new character.) "Well, hell. So what? Grandma Ronan carried a baby in her teeth, and you're upset about what? The ladies at the story time were mean to you? Your friend Nancy won your award? Let's cut the garbage. Answer me this. Look at him. Do you regret it? Be honest. Look at that kid. He's got mucus on his face, ketchup on his shirt. He got into your permanent marker drawer again and he's scribbling over – what is that? – ah, that's the library book you just checked out. He is scribbling all over that book. We're entering day three of his refusal to eat any-thing other than macaroni and cheese, he'll throw a hissy fit at bedtime like he throws at every bed-time, he's a little Lord Fauntleroy, a fat, tow-headed dictator, and I ask you honestly, Do you regret it?"

No. No, I don't. But –

"But what? But it's hard? Life isn't fair? Boo, hoo. You act like you're the first person who's ever had a kid."

I just didn't know it was –

"Well, now you know! Don't you, hot stuff? Now, come on. You can do this. Remember Queens? You took a taxi to that apartment in Queens with no elevator, and the taxi driver dumped your bags on the curb and then drove off, and what'd you do? What'd you do?"

I called the maintenance man.

"That's right. You called the maintenance man. And what happened?"

He didn't answer.

"That's right. So then you started knocking on doors, all along the first floor corridor until you found that Lithuanian grandmother with one of those canes that turns into a stool. And she didn't speak English, but you showed her your baby and all your stuff, and she parked herself on her little cane-stool while you ran that baby in his car seat up five flights of stairs, and you put the baby in the living room and locked the door and went back down and grabbed the suitcase, and then back down five flights for the stroller, and you did it, you managed it, you figured it out. So the question is, what are you going to do now? You can't keep

58

going like you are, you'll go crazy. You're already talking to yourself. You have got to get it together, you've got to pull yourself together and get some balance. We'll start by washing your hair. And put some clean clothes on. And then, you are going out."

But where am I going to go? What about Turk? What'll we do with the kid?

"Figure it out!"

(Wipes face, takes breath.) I get the paper. And before I can even read the headlines, my eyes land on a list of local events, happenings. It's right there. Saturday night. The rec center. Free rentals with ID. It's right there like a neon sign, like a gift.

I call my husband. "Honey, I'm going out Saturday night, you have to watch the kid." Great, he says. Good for you. "Yeah… and I might be going out next Saturday night, too. I might be busy every other Saturday night for the rest of my life. At the rec center. Free rentals with ID. I am going roller-skating!"

I show up by myself. The whole rec center smells like chlorine and feet. The gymnasium is clogged with kids and their mothers. I get my skates – they only have men's sizes. There's no disco ball or Sno Cone machine like I remember from junior high, our local rink.

I haven't worn these in decades. I throw my parka on the bleachers and prepare to stand. My knees were so much better when I did this last. What if I throw out my back? Really, this is stupid. I got a couple hours to myself, I really should be spending this time working on my career. I should be writing, I should be making phone calls, networking or whatever. Instead I'm tottering in a fluorescent gymnasium trying to recapture my youth. As mid-life crises go, this is ridiculous. I should have at least sprung for a sports car. Or a toupee.

I push off. I bend my knees, that's the secret, bend your knees. You don't even have to let the wheels off the ground, just give little pushes with your heel, little pushes. Whoa, steady, stick your butt out, vanity's for suckers. Okay. We're doing it. Ready for a little speed? Hell yes, we're ready.

Round and around I go, as fast as I dare. The lower I go, the faster I go, until pretty soon I'm taking corners like an Olympian. Faster, faster, I'm flying! Brave, fast, free. This gym cannot hold me, even gravity can't hold me, I fly so fast, I am a creature heretofore unknown, an exotic bird that wings around the world! I find myself laughing and smiling at nobody, at everybody. Adrenaline floods my body, my left knee is on fire but I don't care, I'm going to be stiff and sore tomorrow but it's worth it, it's all worth it, and as I fling my body around, the solution hits me, is revealed to me like angels have draped a glorious banner across my path with the message emblazoned in letters of fire and wind and light:

I need a babysitter!

I go roller-skating every week. Saturday nights become sacrosanct. It's like a little piece of turf that I have claimed for England, a tiny oasis of pure pleasure. I'm energized, revitalized. And I start to figure it out.

I get wily with him. "Turk, put your pants on, honey. Put your pants on. Turk. Let's have a race! Who can put their pants on fastest? Winner gets a marshmallow!" I'm handing out marshmallows like vitamins. Let's not tell his doctor.

I bring my laptop everywhere we go and I crank out the pages. I learn to type with one hand. I type when he's on the toilet. I type when I'm on the toilet. I type when I wash dishes. I type in the dark, when I can't see the keyboard and I type in the sun, when I can't see the screen. I type, and I type, and I type.

They say that kids grow up so fast you should treasure these moments. In the almost three years he's been alive, I have watched Turk change so quickly, I want to hold onto him. I want to put his childhood in a jar.

But what's also true is I've changed just as much as he has. And I'm never going back to normal. This is normal.

I had this skirt when I was fourteen that looked like the skirt Winona Ryder wore in the movie Heathers. I wore it with my matching shoes, and I felt like Winona Ryder for about six whole weeks. Then puberty hit. And I inherited my mother's proud childbearing hips.

But I held onto it. Until one day, I'm twenty-nine years old, packing up my apartment, and I come across this skirt. This Winona Ryder skirt. And I do the math and realize I've been carting this thing around with me for sixteen years. I've moved it a total of eleven times. That's eleven separate times I found the skirt in my closet, stuck it in a suitcase, moved it – sometimes across the country – gave it its very own hanger – and for all that time, I wore it not once. I outgrew it almost immediately, but I held onto it, in complete denial, for a decade and a half.

And what was I holding onto, really? The part of me, the fourteen-year-old part who still wanted to be Winona Ryder. Winona is cool? I am not cool. I am a big spaz. Winona shoots arched glances at her love interests? I don't know how to shoot an arched glance. When I try to shoot an arched glance, I look like my contact turned inside out. Winona is a lynx. I am a golden retriever.

A baby is born in a few tough hours, but a mother's birth takes years.

His third birthday approaches, and I think about what to get him. He really likes trucks, but I decide to get him something from which we will both benefit: It's called Pre-School.

Does it get easier? I don't know. And I don't know if "easy" is the right question. Maybe it's not about ease. Maybe ease is a myth sprung from our reliance on painkillers and Netflix instant streaming. Maybe if it's easy, it's not worth as much.

The other night I watch Turk in the bath-tub. And he has momentarily forgotten I'm alive. His boats are in a traffic jam, and as the designated police officer on the scene, it's his job to sort them out and give the captains tickets. He prattles this narrative, oblivious to me, teaching his boats the manners he himself just learned.

"You boats! You have to take turns. You have to be patient!" How many times have I said that to him? How many times have I said that to myself?

"You boats! You say thank you!" I get so worried about how hard it is, I lose sight of how improbable is his existence. This creature, this boy, this child of mine. He makes me laugh and he makes me cry. He is my son. *(Realization.)* And I am his mother!

"Mama! The people are overboard! We have to rescue them!" I do these things, give him these things. I want to give him these things. Give him everything.

It's the parent's job to love their children and it's the children's job to be loved. And this has been going on since forever. A long line of loving and giving and struggle and joy, all of us over-board, fighting for our lives and the lives of our children, we figure it as we splash and swim and haul ass to the shoreline. We strike out toward the mud bank, eyes forward, carrying our legacy any way we can. I do it for him. And someday, if he's lucky, he'll do it for someone else.

I should teach him to swim. Just in case.

END OF PLAY.

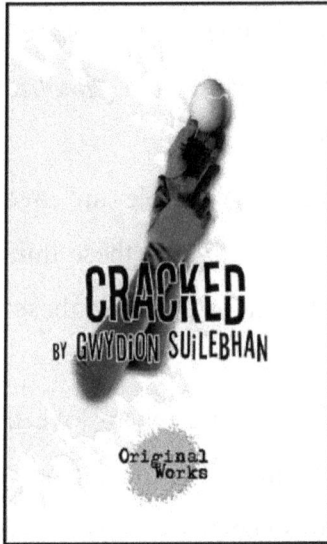

Cracked by Gwydion Suilebhan

Synopsis: Just another episode of a run-of-the-mill cooking show transforms into an intricate, otherworldly grief ritual as the program's hostess — or is she some kind of middle-class priestess? — devises increasingly elaborate ways in which to defer the simple act of cracking an egg. When it's finally time for the demonstration, will she actually be able to just… let go?

Cast Size: 1 Female

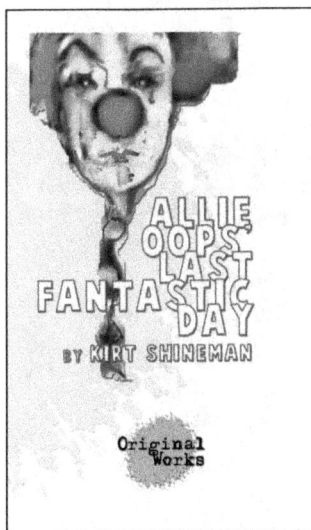

Allie Oops' Last Fantastic Day by Kirt Shineman

Synopsis: While Sue, a mother, waits for the doctor to call for oncology results, she prepares for her son's last year of high school. As is their tradition, Sue attends the first day of school as a clown, Allie Oop, to bring in the new year, but this year, this day, is not as fantastic as she would hope. With the help of her humor and bag of tricks she fools even the toughest foe.

Cast Size: 1 Female

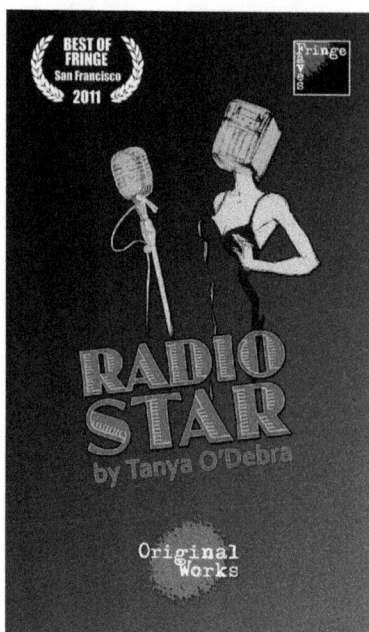

<u>Radio Star</u> by Tanya O'Debra

Synopsis: Radio Star is a 1940's radio detective spoof. In The Case of the Long Distance Lover, Nick McKitrick; Private Dick, is hired by femme fatale Fanny LaRue to find her husband's killer. The plot is a standard mystery, but Radio Star's contemporary sense of humor sets it apart from the pack. A laugh out loud radio romp, easily produced with one actress or a larger cast.

Cast Size: 1 Female

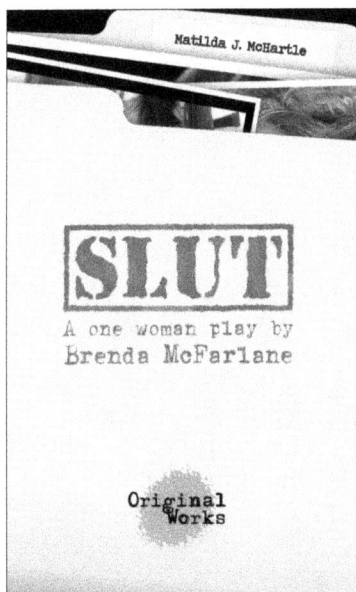

Matilda J. McHartle

SLUT

A one woman play by
Brenda McFarlane

Original
Works

Slut by Brenda McFarlane

Synopsis: Matilda McHartle would describe herself as a perfectly ordinary person and her behavior as completely normal for a single woman in her thirties. She'd admit to being a little quirky for an accountant but she'd never guess what other people might call her if they knew the details of her sex life... that is until she is arrested for running a brothel and taken downtown for formal questioning.

Cast Size: 1 Female

NOTES

NOTES

www.ingramcontent.com/pod-product-compliance
Lightning Source LLC
Chambersburg PA
CBHW060159070426
42447CB00033B/2214